DoodleLoops
Writing

written and illustrated by

Sandy Baker

To view all books in the DoodleLoops series, please visit DoodleLoops.com.

For bulk purchases of DoodleLoops books or any other inquiries, please contact us at info@ doodleloops.com.

A Word About DoodleLoops Writing

The DoodleLoops included in this book are unique learning tools. They involve little or no teacher preparation and offer incredible results. The stimulating, though-provoking illustrations naturally lead the children into the world of creative writing. Used during your writing instruction, DoodleLoops Writing offers enrichment for all ability levels. They afford you the opportunity to teach sentence structure, the elements of a story, the use of descriptive words, spelling, punctuation and so much more! And above all, they stimulate creative thinking! What a sense of accomplishment you'll feel as you see your students' writing skills grow dramatically over the course of a year.

DoodleLoops Writing is best for children at the preschool level through the fourth grade.

Directions for Use

The <u>DoodleLoops Writing</u> program spans a number of grade levels and can be used with beginning as well as advanced writers. We have included directions for Beginning Writers as well as Advanced Writers. Choose the directions that are appropriate for your students.

Directions for Beginning Writers

How To Begin

1. Use a demonstration <u>DoodleLoops Writing</u> page (p.1) to introduce the DoodleLoops concept.

2. Display the DoodleLoops page in clear view of all of the students. Read the question, "Who am I?" to the class. Then let the children brainstorm ideas in sentence form, such as, "I am a monster." "I am an alien." "I am a scary space creature."

3. Choose one of the sentences, such as, "I am a monster." Spend a substantial amount of time discussing how to "sound out" the words that the children don't already know how to spell. Emphasize that any spelling is acceptable. List the children's spelling suggestions on the board or on chart paper, such as:

"I am a mnstr."

"I am a mnr."

"I m a mnsr."

(Correct spelling skills are, of course, important, and you may wish to edit the children's work later. However, allowing the children to spell the words as they hear them when they tackle new DoodleLoops encourages their creative writing skills and allows their ideas to flow.)

4. Distribute the first <u>DoodleLoops Writing</u> page to the children. Tell them to use their imaginations and to think of many possibilities before beginning to write. Encourage them to take their time, work carefully and come up with their own unique ideas. At first, expect a short sentence or two from the majority of the children. However, if you have advanced writers in your class, encourage them to write more complex descriptions or stories. It is very important to encourage the children as they tackle their first DoodleLoops. It is helpful to circulate throughout the class as the children write, offering praise and assistance.

Expectations

1. It is important to continually encourage the children to:

   - think of many possibilities for stories or descriptions before beginning to write

   - think of unique ideas

   - work neatly and carefully

   - leave appropriate spaces between their words

2. As the year progresses, encourage your students to write longer and more detailed stories. You may use DoodleLoops to teach the following:

   - proper capitalization and punctuation

   - use of descriptive words

   - how to write a complete story, including a beginning, middle and end

   - spelling skills

   - and more!

3. Optional: You may wish to write the correct spelling above the misspelled words the children write on their DoodleLoops. The correct spelling is provided to help improve their spelling skills and in order to help the children remember what they have written so that they may reread their work and share it with their families and classmates.

Directions for Advanced Writers

How to Begin

1. Use a demonstration <u>DoodleLoops Writing</u> page (p.1) to introduce the DoodleLoops concept:

2. Display the DoodleLoops page in clear view of all of the students. Read the question, "Who am I?" to the class. Let the children brainstorm ideas, and list them on the board or on chart paper.

3. Choose one idea from the list. Discuss various ways to expand the idea into a story (with a beginning, middle and end) or a descriptive narrative. Using the board or on chart paper, model an example of each.

~DoodleLoops~

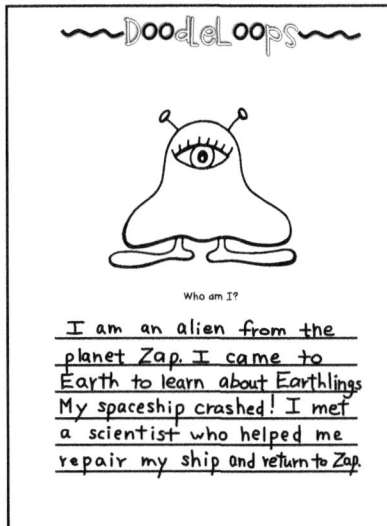

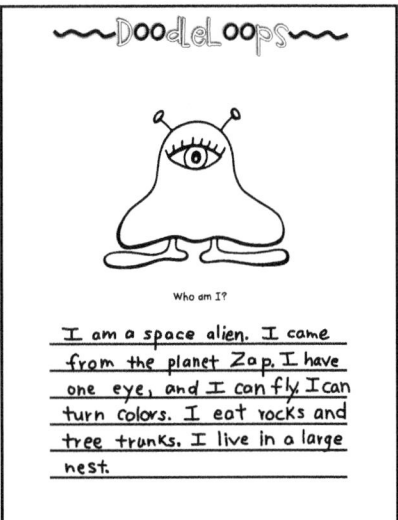

Your models may be longer and much more elaborate and detailed, depending upon the ability level of your students.

4. Distribute the first DoodleLoops page to the children. Tell them to use their imaginations and to think of many possibilities before beginning to write. Encourage them to take their time, work carefully and come up with their own unique ideas.

Expectations

1. As the year progresses, encourage your students to write longer and more detailed stories. For children who need additional paper, a master of lined paper is provided at the back of this book.

2. You may use the DoodleLoops to introduce more advanced skills, such as:

   - the use of proper punctuation and capitalization

   - the use of commas

   - the use of quotation marks

   - character development

   - paragraph formation

   - different types of writing, such as persuasive, narrative, poetry, etc.

   - research skills

   - and so much more!

   Each time you wish to introduce a new skill, use a DoodleLoops page to model your expectations.

3. Conferencing: In order to help your children become more proficient writers, you may find it helpful to conference with them from time to time.

The Importance of Sharing

1. It is important that the children have a vehicle for sharing their DoodleLoops in order to reinforce their ideas, to have support and feedback from their classmates and to encourage divergent thinking.

2. The children may share their work in a variety of ways. You may choose one or more of the following:

- Share the DoodleLoops as a group. If time allows, each child may share his or her DoodleLoops with the class. If not, a small number of children may share daily, so that over the course of a week all of the children have had a turn to share.

- Share with a partner. You may pair up your children or put them in small groups and ask them to share with one another and offer praise and support for each other's work.

- Display the DoodleLoops on a bulletin board in the room or in the hallway so that other students can read them.

- You may wish to have your class or a group of your students share their DoodleLoops with another classroom.

- You may create a slideshow of the DoodleLoops on the computer.

- Share the DoodleLoops online. Scan or take a photo of the finished DoodleLoops, and post them to the gallery at DoodleLoops.com or to your classroom social media accounts.

- Share with family. Scan or take a photo of the finished DoodleLoops, and email them directly to family members and friends.

- Share with us! Scan or take a photo of your finished DoodleLoops. Email them to info@doodleloops.com with the subject "Sample" and we will post them on our site! (Parental permission is required.)

Evaluation

1. <u>DoodleLoops Writing</u> gives a good indication of the development of the children's writing skills, as well as their ability to express their thoughts and ideas clearly.

2. <u>DoodleLoops Writing</u> also give a good indication of the development of the children's phonetic and spelling skills.

3. If you wish to keep a record of the children's progress in the areas of writing and language arts, DoodleLoops are perfect for portfolio assessment.

Across the Curriculum Usage and Cooperative Learning

1. DoodleLoops may be used to reinforce skills being taught in other subject areas. You may use the DoodleLoops provided to tie in with:

- Holidays (Halloween, Thanksgiving, Valentine's Day, etc.)
- Affective Education (feelings, emotions and self-esteem)
- Family Relationships
- Community
- Homes
- Transportation
- Geography
- Environments
- Weather and Seasons
- Outer Space
- The Senses
- Plants
- Animals
- Insects

There is also a DoodleLoops page at the end of this book which has no illustration. You may use this page to insert any picture you wish that relates to any special subject matter that you may be teaching.

©**Sandy Baker**
Writing

Optional: You may also allow the children to create their own DoodleLoops using the blank DoodleLoops page.

2. DoodleLoops may also be used as a cooperative learning tool. You may ask two or three children to work on a DoodleLoops page together.

Directions For Use At Home

Follow the directions for school use, and you will be able to easily adapt these directions in order to share these wonderful learning tools with your children at home!

Enjoy DoodleLoops!

They offer endless possibilities for learning
and for expanding creative awareness!

Contact Us!

Tell us how you've been using our DoodleLoops books:
info@doodleloops.com
www.DoodleLoops.com

Writing

Student Samples

To view more completed samples in full color, please visit:
DoodleLoops.com/gallery/

~~DoodleLoops~~

~DoodleLoops~

Who am I?

~DoodleLoops~

Home run
Ball. hom ran
Home run
jack! hom ran
jack. jack you.
won
won the game!
game

~DoodleLoops~

Who am I?

discombobulated
You are a
Dis ki Bo Be tad
Baseball player.
about
you o are about
hit
to hatt the

Writing

DoodleLoops

What am I cooking?

Soup
Sop   piy (Pie)
one Day (day)
a man
name nd (named)
Tom richrdson (Richardson)
wrkt (worked) at
the Best (best) rest rono (restaurant)
1

©Sandy Baker
Writing

DoodleLoops.com

~~DoodleLoops~~

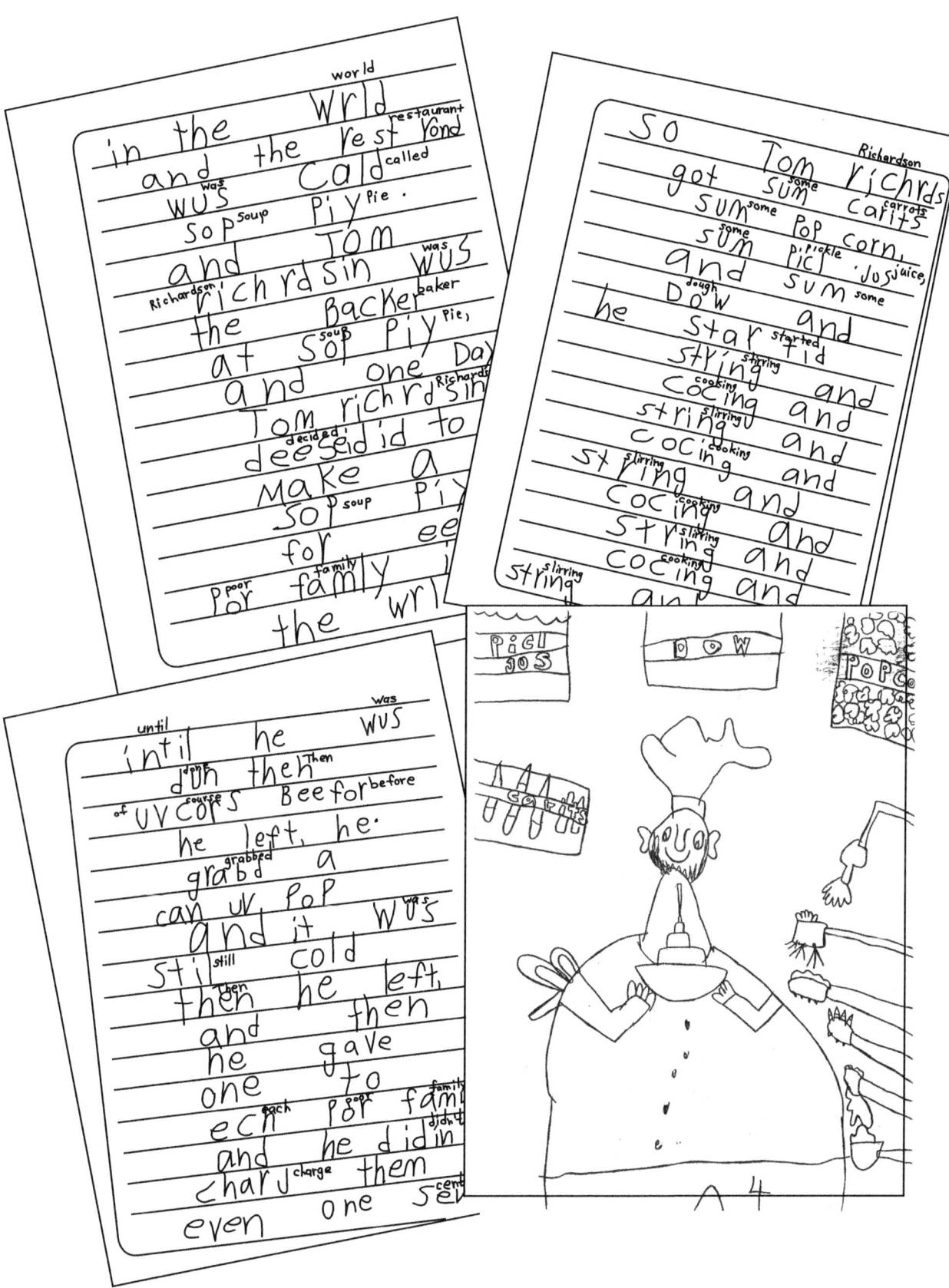

©Sandy Baker
Writing

DoodleLoops

~DoodleLoops~

Then
then he gave nursing
ech each nrsing
home in the
wrld 5
world
then he
Then
saed to
said in
evre onr
every owner
of eech nrsin
each nursing
home, "I don't
eevens
need sen
one cen

and then
Tom richrd sin
richardson
ce pt kept
kept
wacing and
walking
wacing and
walking
wocing and
walking
wocing and
walking
wocing and
walking
wocing and
walking
wocing and
walking
wocing and
walking
wocing and
walking
then Tom
richrd sin
richardson
was Bak
back
to sop piy
soup pie

DoodleLoops

Who Am I?

I am a cobl aleen and I am frendl ee. I have big feet and a big ay.

©Sandy Baker
Writing

1

Why am I so happy?

_____

_____

_____

_____

_____

DoodleLoops

Why am I crying?

_____

_____

_____

_____

_____

Writing

3

What do I see?

I see the sun and
The sun is Bright.

DoodleLoops

Who am I?

_____

_____

_____

_____

_____

Writing

5

What do I smell?

I smell some yumy buootast soop.

DoodleLoops

What do I hear?

_____

_____

_____

_____

_____

©Sandy Baker
Writing

DoodleLoops

What am I dreaming about?

_____

_____

_____

_____

_____

©Sandy Baker
Writing

Who am I?

I am mrs cllumseo
clain.

Writing

9

What am I?

A dellishas berger
with a paty chees
ans green letese.

DoodleLoops

Who am I?

A Abnana ccunseu
hood

©Sandy Baker
Writing

11

Who am I?

___ hot bio litle
clumse o hot .

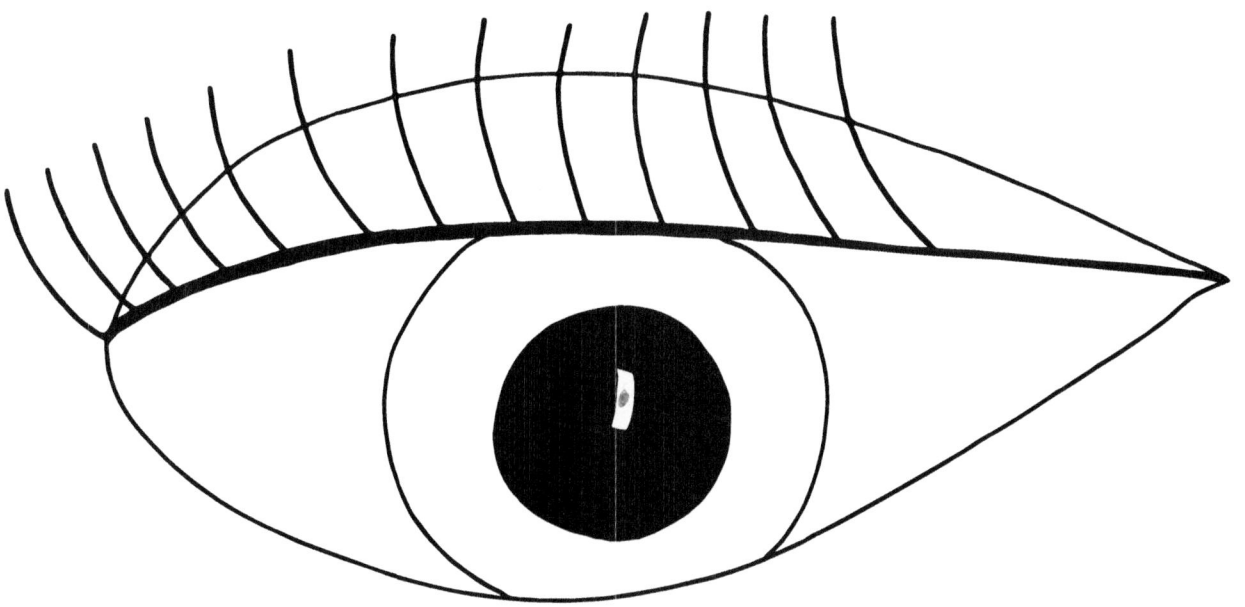

What am I?

A Lolly bloy eye.
A Lolly eye as bloy
as The sceye.

Who am I?

_____

_____

_____

_____

_____

DoodleLoops

not make it yet!

Who am I?

A big ttt lll eyh boy.

15

Who am I?

_____

_____

_____

_____

_____

DoodleLoops

What is inside?

The Bakcree wiv
sum donuts ond
thoy are sweet
and sugary.

Writing

DoodleLoops

Who is behind this door?

_____

_____

_____

_____

_____

Who are we?

_____

_____

_____

_____

©**Sandy Baker**
Writing

Who am I?

_____

mir screee bat
hed on cup v
bats.

_____

©**Sandy Baker**
Writing

DoodleLoops

What's in the pot?

_____

_____

_____

_____

_____

Writing

DoodleLoops

Who am I?

_____

_____

_____

_____

_____

©Sandy Baker
Writing

DoodleLoops.com

Who lives here?

_____

_____

_____

_____

_____

What is in my hat?

_____

_____

_____

_____

_____

DoodleLoops

Who are we?

_____

_____

_____

_____

_____

Who am I?

_____

_____

_____

_____

_____

Who am I?

_____

_____

_____

_____

_____

Who are we?

_____

_____

_____

_____

_____

Who am I?

_____

_____

_____

_____

_____

Writing

What am I cooking?

DoodleLoops.com

Who am I?

_____

_____

_____

_____

_____

Writing

Who am I?

_____

up sid doшn

sno mon

_____

_____

_____

DoodleLoops

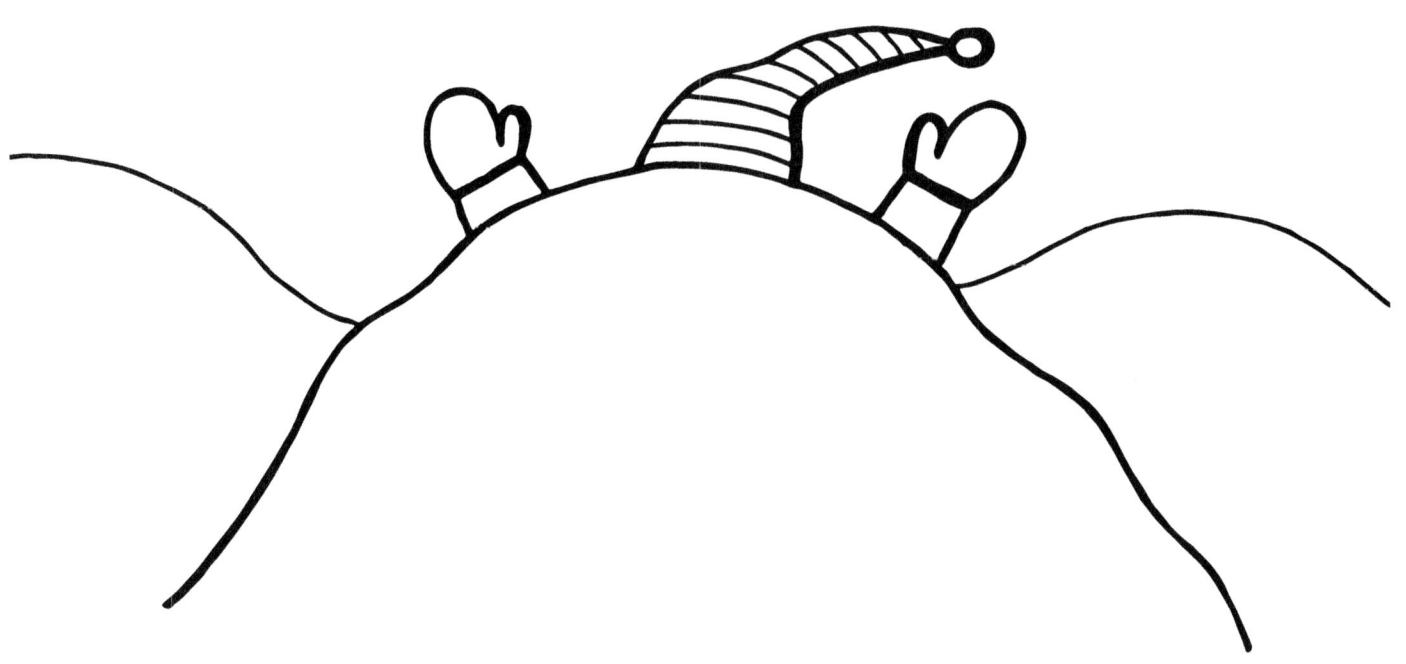

Who am I?

_____

_____

_____

_____

_____

Writing

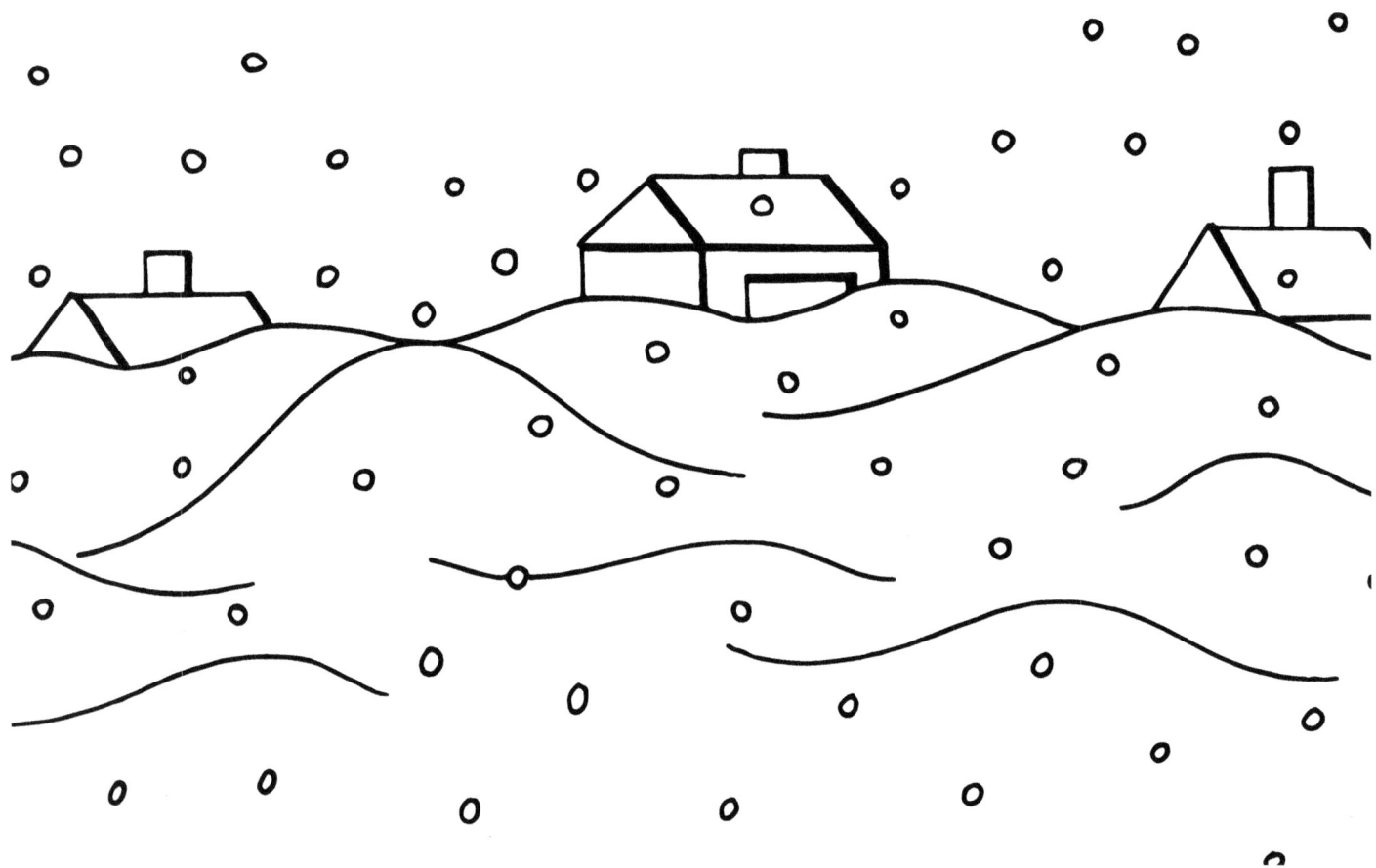

What is happening?

_____

_____

_____

_____

_____

©Sandy Baker
Writing

What am I thinking about?

_____

_____

_____

_____

_____

©Sandy Baker
Writing

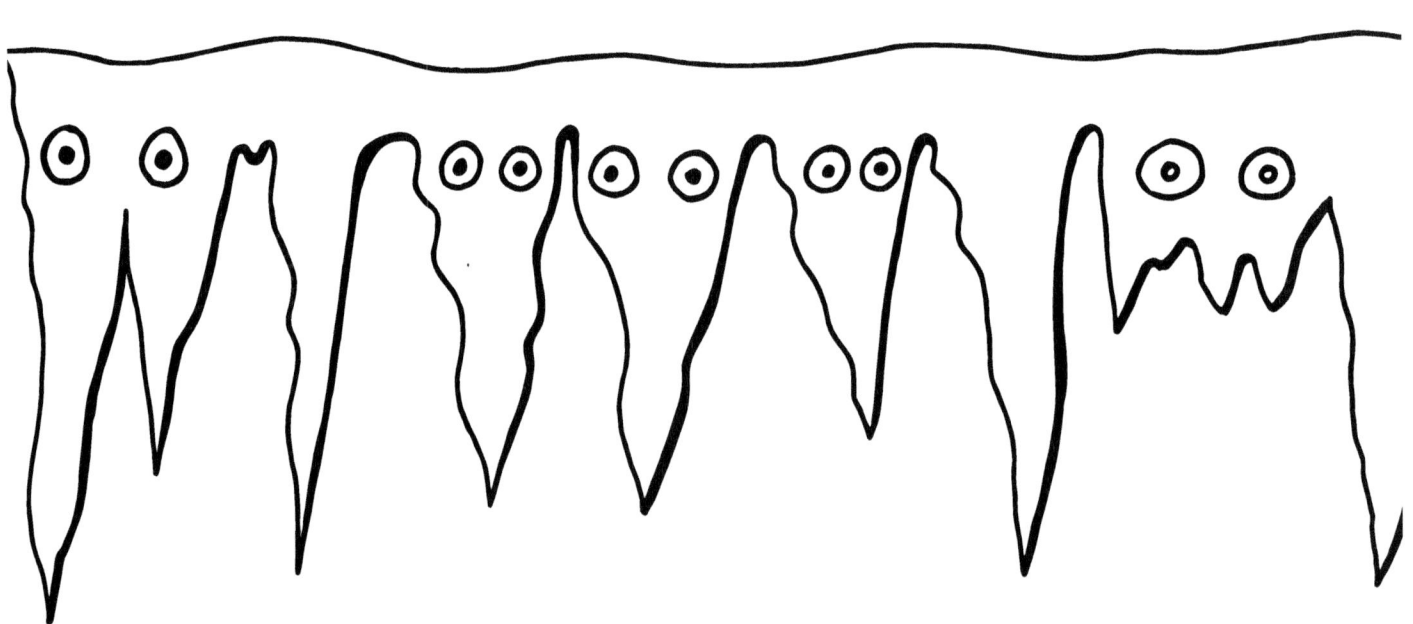

Who are we?

_____

_____

_____

_____

_____

Who are we?

The hart fomcea
or 4 horts.

Who am I?

_____

_____

_____

_____

_____

DoodleLoops

Where are we going?

_____

_____

_____

_____

_____

Writing

Who am I?

_____

_____

_____

_____

_____

What do I see?

_____

_____

_____

_____

_____

DoodleLoops

Who are we?

_____

_____

_____

_____

_____

©Sandy Baker
Writing

DoodleLoops

What am I?

A aleeoon if or
aleeoons eron
soons.

Writing

Who are we?

The moon blest.

DoodleLoops

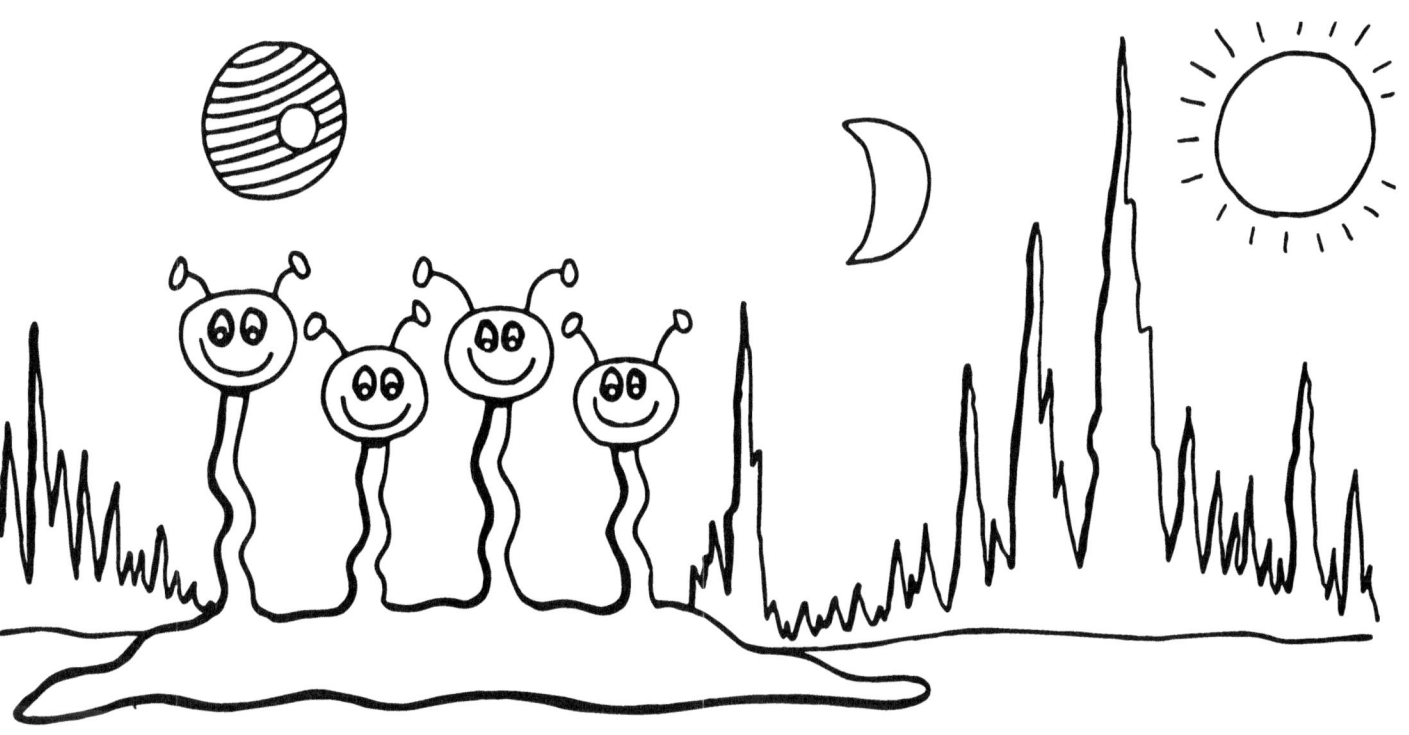

Where are we?

_____

_____

_____

_____

_____

~~DoodleLoops~~

Who am I?

_____

_____

_____

_____

_____

Who are we?

frend slapys.

DoodeLoops

What am I?

_____

_____

_____

_____

_____

©Sandy Baker
Writing

Who am I?

_____

_____

_____

_____

_____

©**Sandy Baker**
Writing

What am I?

_____

_____

_____

_____

_____

DoodleLoops

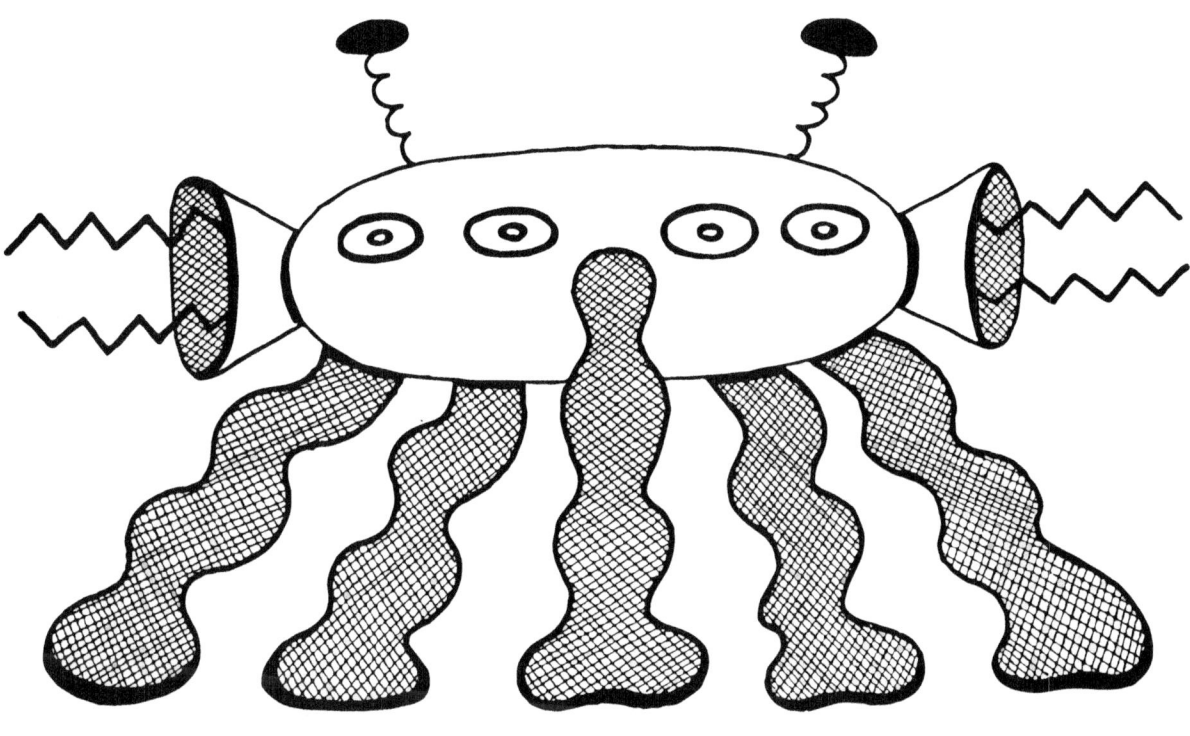

Who am I?

_____

_____

_____

_____

_____

Writing

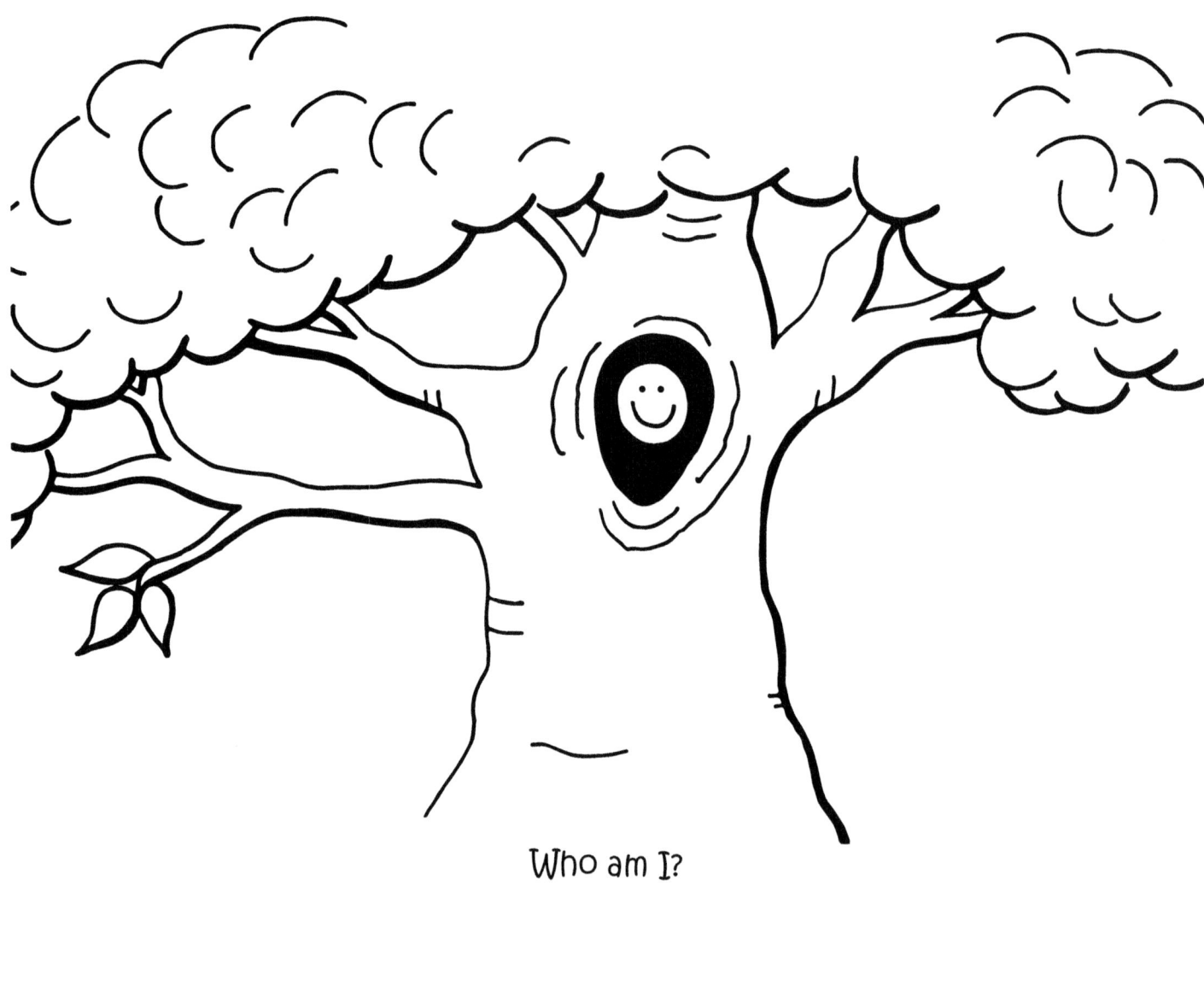

Who am I?

_____

_____

_____

_____

_____

DoodleLoops

Where am I?

_____

_____

_____

_____

_____

©Sandy Baker
Writing

Where am I?

_____

_____

_____

_____

_____

DoodleLoops

Where am I?

_____

_____

_____

_____

_____

Writing

DoodleLoops

Where am I?

_____

_____

_____

_____

_____

DoodleLoops.com

DoodleLoops

What am I? What is inside of me?

_____

_____

_____

_____

_____

©Sandy Baker
Writing

DoodleLoops

What is this place?

_____

_____

_____

_____

_____

DoodleLoops.com

Where am I?

Not bot in tho
forist nt tho drs
DE.

Writing

DoodleLoops

What is happening?

_____

_____

_____

_____

_____

DoodleLoops

What is happening?

_____

_____

_____

_____

_____

What is happening?

_____

_____

_____

_____

_____

What is happening?

_____

_____

_____

_____

_____

Writing

DoodleLoops

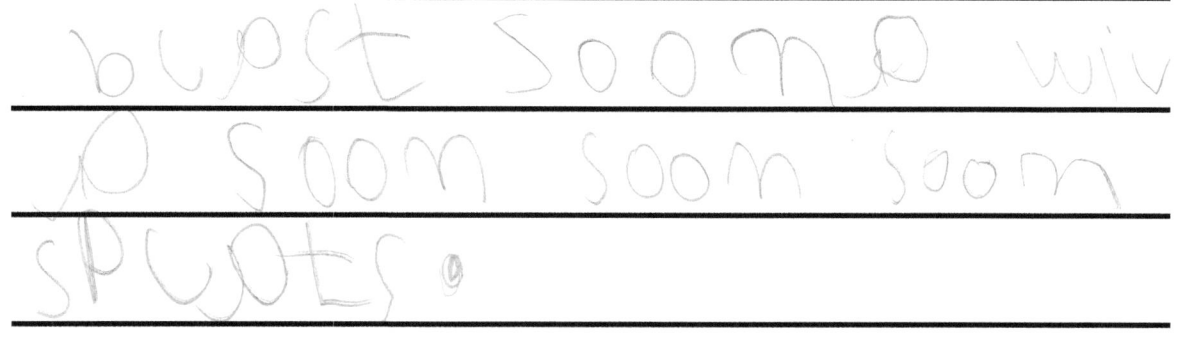

Who am I?

_____

blast soome wiv

d soom soom soom

spoots.

_____

What am I?

Where am I going?

_____

_____

_____

_____

_____

DoodleLoops

Where am I going?

_____

_____

_____

_____

_____

©Sandy Baker
Writing

DoodLeLoops

Who are we? Where are we going?

_____

_____

_____

_____

_____

DoodleLoops

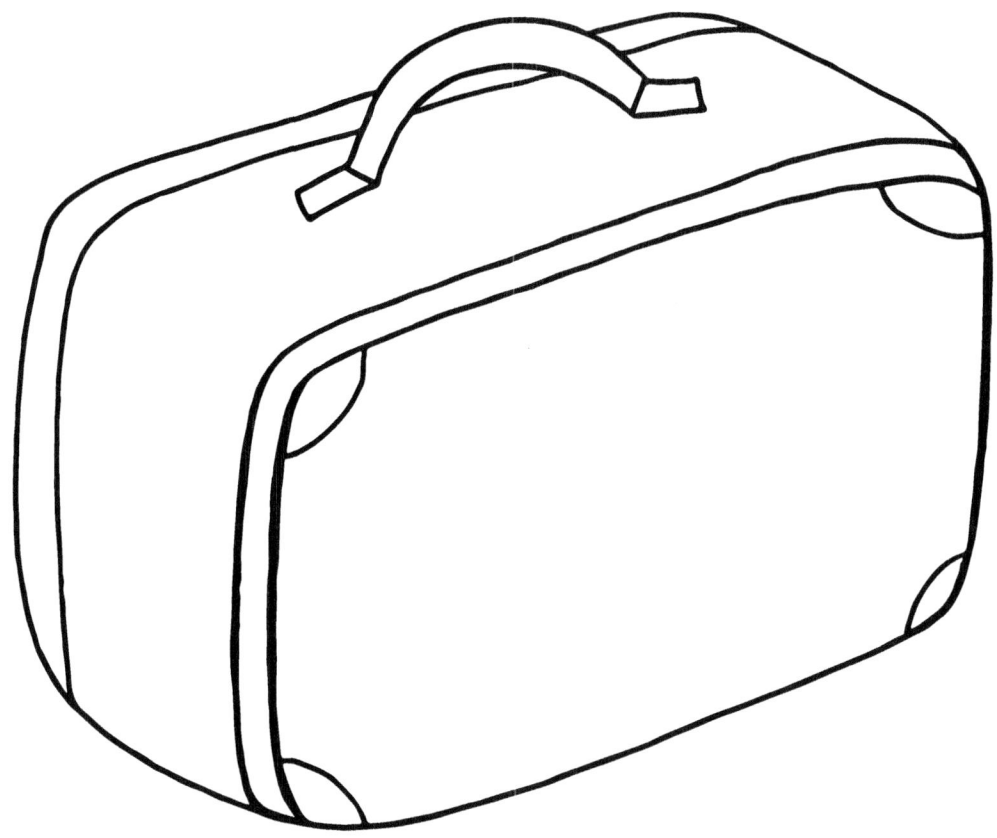

What is inside of me?

_____

_____

_____

_____

_____

©Sandy Baker
Writing

DoodleLoops

Who lives here?

A queen i wer in g a byootfiiel krown at is shiny and sparkle o o

DoodleLoops

Who lives here?

_____

_____

_____

_____

_____

©Sandy Baker
Writing

DoodleLoops

Who lives here?

_____

_____

_____

_____

_____

©Sandy Baker
Writing

DoodleLoops

What is this?

_____

_____

_____

_____

_____

Who am I?

_____

_____

_____

_____

_____

| ©Sandy Baker
Writing

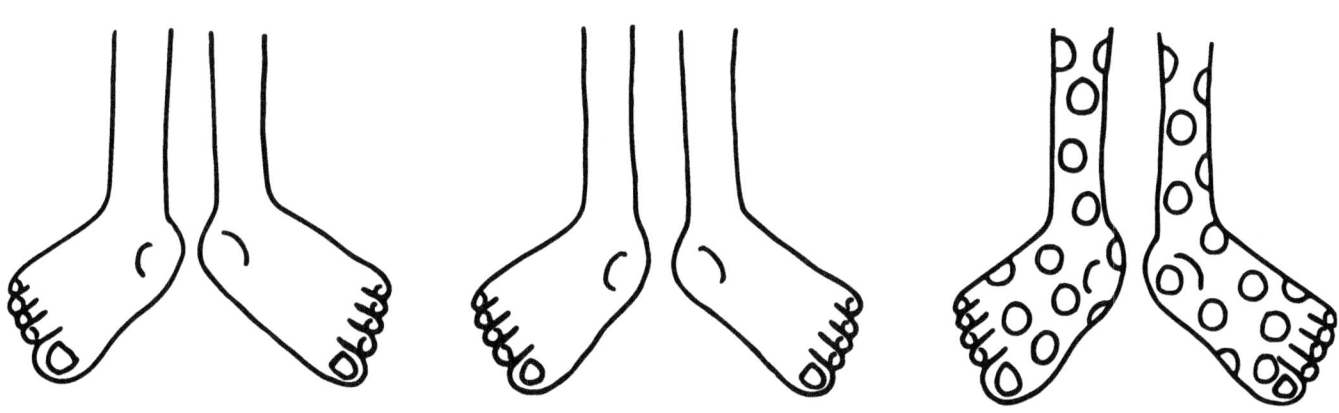

What are we?

_____

_____

_____

_____

_____

Who am I?

_____

_____

_____

_____

_____

©Sandy Baker
Writing

What is happening?

_____

_____

_____

_____

_____

DoodleLoops

Who are we?

_____

_____

_____

_____

_____

©**Sandy Baker**
Writing

DoodleLoops.com

Who am I?

_____

_____

_____

_____

_____

©Sandy Baker
Writing

DoodleLoops

What is inside?

_____

_____

_____

_____

_____

©**Sandy Baker**
Writing

Who are we?

_____

_____

_____

_____

_____

What am I?

_____

_____

_____

_____

_____

Writing

DoodleLoops

Who am I?

_____

_____

_____

_____

_____

Writing

What am I reading about?

_____

_____

_____

_____

_____

DoodleLoops

What am I reading about?

_____

_____

_____

_____

_____

©Sandy Baker | 85
Writing

DoodleLoops

What am I reading about?

_____

_____

_____

_____

_____

What is in here?

_____

_____

_____

_____

_____

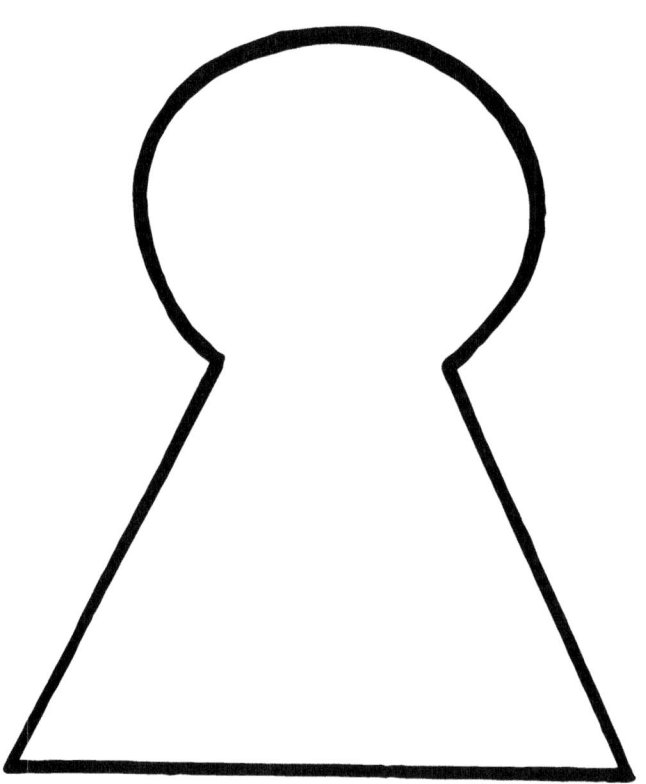

I am a keyhole. What do you see through me?

_____

_____

_____

_____

_____

What is this pointing to?

_____

_____

_____

_____

_____

DoodleLoops

Who am I?

_____

_____

_____

_____

_____

Writing

What do I see?

_____

_____

_____

_____

_____

What do we see?

_____

_____

_____

_____

_____

©**Sandy Baker**
Writing

Who am I?

_____

_____

_____

_____

_____

Who am I?

_____

_____

_____

_____

_____

Writing

DoodleLoops

Who am I?

_____

_____

_____

_____

_____

©Sandy Baker
Writing

95

DoodleLoops

Who am I?

_____

_____

_____

_____

_____

Who am I?

_____

_____

_____

_____

_____

DoodleLoops

Who am I?

_____

_____

_____

_____

_____

©Sandy Baker
Writing

DoodleLoops.com

DoodleLoops

Who am I?

_____

_____

_____

_____

_____

DoodleLoops

What am I?

_____

_____

_____

_____

_____

©Sandy Baker
Writing

Moo!

Who am I?

_____

_____

_____

_____

_____

Writing

DoodleLoops

Who am I?

_____

_____

_____

_____

_____

©Sandy Baker
Writing

DoodleLoops

Who are we?

_____

_____

_____

_____

_____

Writing

Who am I?

_____

_____

_____

_____

_____

©**Sandy Baker**
Writing

What am I?

_____

_____

_____

_____

_____

DoodleLoops

Who are we?

_____

_____

_____

_____

_____

What do I see?

_____

_____

_____

_____

_____

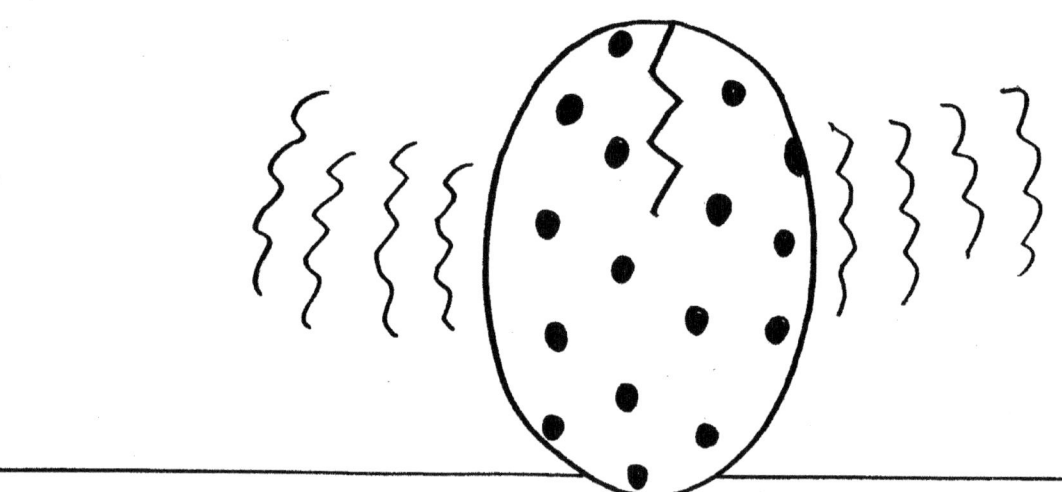

What is happening?

_____

_____

_____

_____

_____

Where am I going?

_____

_____

_____

_____

DoodleLoops

Where are we going?

_____

_____

_____

_____

_____

Writing

_____

_____

_____

_____

_____

DoodleLoops

©**Sandy Baker**
Writing

Printed in Great Britain
by Amazon

83226986R00079